# Tapestry Of Life

*by*

Abir Chakraborty

# Tapestry Of Life
## by Abir Chakraborty

Copyright © 2024

All Rights reserved.



ISBN: 978-93-62768-62-9

Published by

**DOUBLE 9 BOOKS**
2/13-B, Ansari Road
Daryaganj, New Delhi – 110002
info@double9books.com
www.double9books.com
Tel. 011-40042856

# ABOUT THE AUTHOR

Abir Chakraborty, an eighth-grade student at Lakshmipat Singhania Academy, is a budding author with a passion for enhancing readers' interest and vocabulary. Through his writing, he aims to captivate audiences and expand their linguistic horizons. With creativity and dedication, Abir utilizes his talent to craft engaging narratives that leave a lasting impact on his readers. As he continues to develop his skills, his literary contributions are sure to inspire and entertain audiences of all ages.

# CONTENTS

# OVERVIEW

A PERSON ADDS A LOT TO THE CANVAS OF EXISTENCE , PEOPLE CREATE A BOND AND EXPERIENCE UPS AND DOWNS ALSO.

Every person adds to the palette of life on the enormous canvas of existence, creating a distinct and elaborate tapestry of relationships, experiences, and feelings. This book invites readers to consider the intricacy and beauty of the composition of their own lives as it delves into the vivid hues that accentuate our journey.

In this book, we want to explore and talk about how amazing and interesting this artwork called "life" is. We want you to think about all the cool and different things that make your life special. It's like looking at a big, colorful painting and realizing that each part has its own story and importance.

So, we're going to learn about the different feelings we have, the things we do, and the people we know. All of these things together create a beautiful and complicated picture that is just like a big, wonderful tapestry. We want you to understand that your life is like a fantastic piece of art, and the artist who makes it so amazing!

Life is like a big story, and every person is an important character in that story. When we think about life, we can imagine it as a big puzzle where each piece is a person. Every person does things and makes choices, just like you do every day. Sometimes, these choices and actions can have a special and important effect on other people. It's a bit like when you drop a stone into a pond, and it makes ripples that spread out. Similarly, the things we do and the way we treat others can create ripples in the big pond of life. Even if we don't realize it, the choices we make can leave a mark and become a part of the bigger picture of all people everywhere. So, it's important to remember that each of us is like a tiny but powerful puzzle piece, making the big picture of life interesting and beautiful.

Life is the state of being alive, characterized by various activities, experiences, and the presence of living organisms. It encompasses the conditions, events, and phenomena that distinguish living entities from inanimate matter. Life involves growth, reproduction, response to stimuli, and adaptation to the environment. It is a continuous journey filled with a diverse range of emotions, relationships, and experiences. Life is not only about individual existence but also about the interconnectedness of living beings, contributing to the intricate tapestry of existence. It is a dynamic and ever-changing phenomenon, marked by the passage of time and the constant evolution of living organisms and their surroundings.

Life is a wonderful journey filled with moments, experiences, and emotions. Imagine life as a colorful adventure, where each day is a new page waiting to be written. We are like storytellers, weaving our tales through laughter, tears, and everything in between. From the moment we are born, we start painting the canvas of our existence with the vibrant palette of our choices.

In this grand tapestry of life, we form connections with others—family, friends, and those we meet along the way. These relationships add depth and meaning, turning the ordinary into extraordinary. Life is a mosaic of joy and challenges, like a rollercoaster ride with twists and turns that shape our character and resilience.

WE HOPE YOU WILL LIKE THE BOOK.

# CHAPTER 1
# THE CANVAS OPENS

Once upon a time, in the enchanting world of wonder and magic, the expansive canvas of life beckoned to be woven into an intricate tapestry of stories. This canvas, resembling a colossal book, unfolded its pages with each person contributing a distinctive and cherished chapter to its narrative.

The canvas began its journey as a blank slate upon the arrival of a newborn. As the little one grew, the tender strokes of family and friends began to grace the canvas, imprinting it with the earliest hues of laughter, hugs, and the occasional teardrop—the beginnings of a captivating life story.

With the passage of years, the canvas blossomed into a kaleidoscope of colors, each day adding new adventures and valuable lessons. Friends, akin to vibrant markers, embellished the journey, infusing it with excitement and companionship. In the vast expanse, challenges arose, casting shadows like dark clouds in the sky. Yet, akin to the reassuring promise of the sun following rain, joyous moments unfailingly followed the trials.

This canvas was no solitary tale; it evolved into a grand painting featuring myriad characters. People intertwined their stories, forming a web of kindness and love that illuminated the canvas with radiant sparks. Every act of sharing and caring became a luminous twinkle, enhancing the brilliance of the collective life narrative.

Just as the pages turned in a book, the seasons changed within this magical world. Childhood marked the commencement, filled with boundless curiosity and playful endeavors. The teenage years introduced fresh colors of discovery and growth, while adulthood represented the middle of the story—a blend of responsibilities and dreams merging seamlessly.

In this mystical realm, every action possessed a unique power. Acts of kindness and love acted as magic spells, casting a spell of joy and happiness upon all who encountered them. Dreams and goals were akin to stars in the night sky, guiding individuals on their unique paths.

As the canvas continued its unfolding, each person left an indelible mark. Their stories intertwined, creating a breathtaking masterpiece that celebrated the beauty found in differences. The canvas of life became a perpetual adventure, with surprises and treasures concealed in every corner, waiting to be uncovered.

And so, the tale of the canvas persisted, with each person contributing their own distinct narrative. The magic of this world lay in shared laughter, extended helping hands, and the love that painted the canvas in the most extraordinary and vibrant ways. As the canvas expanded, the story of life evolved into a timeless masterpiece, cherished by all who embraced its wondrous pages, reflecting the awe-inspiring journey of existence.

## TRY THESE!

**1. What is the canvas in the story?**

      a. A magical world

      b. A book

      c. An intricate tapestry

      d. An enchanted forest

**2. What does the canvas represent in the story?**

      a. A blank slate

      b. A magical spell

      c. A journey of discovery

      d. A hidden treasure

**3. How does the canvas begin its journey?**

      a. As a magical spell

      b. With a newborn

      c. Unfolding its pages

      d. Akin to a dark cloud

**4. What are the earliest hues imprinted on the canvas?**

      a. Sun and rain

      b. Laughter, hugs, and tears

      c. Shadows and challenges

      d. Magic spells

## 5. What do friends represent in the story?

    a. Dark clouds

    b. Boundless curiosity

    c. Vibrant markers

    d. Luminous twinkles

## 6. How does the canvas respond to challenges?

    a. By casting magic spells

    b. With a blend of responsibilities and dreams

    c. Unfailing joyous moments

    d. Like the reassuring promise of the sun after rain

## 7. What does the canvas evolve into?

    a. A grand painting with characters

    b. A dark cloud

    c. A mystical realm

    d. A hidden treasure

## 8. What illuminates the canvas with radiant sparks?

    a. Challenges

    b. Dreams and goals

    c. Acts of sharing and caring

    d. Boundless curiosity

## 9. What marks the commencement of childhood in the story?

    a. Responsibilities

    b. Akin to a dark cloud

    c. Boundless curiosity and play

    d. Luminous twinkles

## 10. What are dreams and goals compared to in the story?

    a. Vibrant markers

    b. Stars in the night sky

    c. Dark clouds

    d. A blend of responsibilities and dreams

**11. What do acts of kindness and love act as in the story?**

    a. Luminous twinkles

    b. Boundless curiosity

    c. Vibrant markers

    d. Magic spells

**12. What is the canvas of life compared to in the story?**

    a. A hidden treasure

    b. A perpetual adventure

    c. An enchanted forest

    d. An intricate tapestry

**13. What do challenges cast shadows like in the story?**

    a. Dark clouds

    b. Luminous twinkles

    c. Vibrant markers

    d. Sun after rain

**14. What does adulthood represent in the story?**

    a. Childhood

    b. Akin to a dark cloud

    c. A blend of responsibilities and dreams

    d. Unfailing joyous moments

**15. What is the magic of this world in the story?**

    a. Shared laughter

    b. Dark clouds

    c. A blend of responsibilities and dreams

    d. Unfailing joyous moments

**16. What guides individuals on their unique paths in the story?**

    a. Shadows and challenges

    b. Vibrant markers

    c. Stars in the night sky

    d. A perpetual adventure

17. **What is the canvas compared to as it continues its unfolding?**

    a. A magical world

    b. A grand painting with characters

    c. A blank slate

    d. An intricate tapestry

18. **How does each person contribute to the canvas in the story?**

    a. With dark clouds

    b. By leaving an indelible mark

    c. Unfolding pages

    d. Casting magic spells

19. **What does the canvas become in the story?**

    a. A timeless masterpiece

    b. An enchanted forest

    c. An intricate tapestry

    d. A blank slate

20. **What is cherished by all who embrace its wondrous pages in the story?**

    a. Magic spells

    b. Acts of sharing and caring

    c. A timeless masterpiece

    d. Unfailing joyous moments

21. **What is hidden in every corner of the canvas in the story?**

    a. Vibrant markers

    b. Luminous twinkles

    c. Surprises and treasures

    d. Dark clouds

22. **What is the canvas painted with in the most extraordinary and vibrant ways in the story?**

    a. Laughter, hugs, and tears

    b. Dreams and goals

    c. Shared laughter, extended helping hands, and love

    d. Challenges

**23. What is the canvas compared to as it expands in the story?**

    a. A hidden treasure

    b. An enchanted forest

    c. A perpetual adventure

    d. A grand painting with characters

**24. What does the canvas celebrate in the story?**

    a. Challenges

    b. The beauty found in differences

    c. Dreams and goals

    d. Acts of sharing and caring

**25. What does every person add to the canvas in the story?**

    a. Vibrant markers

    b. Their own distinct narrative

    c. Luminous twinkles

    d. A blend of responsibilities and dreams

**26. What unfolds its pages with each person contributing to its narrative in the story?**

    a. A grand painting with characters

    b. A magical world

    c. A blank slate

    d. The expansive canvas of life

**27. What is akin to a reassuring promise in the story?**

    a. Vibrant markers

    b. Challenges

    c. Acts of sharing and caring

    d. Unfailing joyous moments

**28. What does the canvas represent at the beginning of the story?**

    a. A blank slate

    b. Akin to a dark cloud

    c. An enchanted forest

    d. A grand painting with characters

29. **What does the canvas unfold with each person contributing a distinctive chapter to in the story?**

    a. A blank slate

    b. A magical world

    c. An intricate tapestry

    d. A grand painting with characters

30. **What does the canvas become as it unfolds in the story?**

    a. A timeless masterpiece

    b. A perpetual adventure

    c. A hidden treasure

    d. An enchanted forest

# CHAPTER 2
# GROWTH RELATED BRUSHSTROKES

Once upon a time in the colorful city of Creativia lived an artist named Lily. Lily had a magic brush that could bring her drawings to life. One day, sitting in her art studio full of rainbow colors, she decided to paint a canvas that represented her own journey of growing up.Lilio dipped her magic brush in bright yellow paint, symbolizing sunny days of happiness. While painting, he remembered the time he learned to ride a bicycle without training wheels. It was successful, adding a warm and happy glow to her fabric.Next, Lily chose the color blue, which reminds her of the challenges she faced. In a decisive stroke, he painted a storm cloud on his canvas to represent failure when he failed to solve a difficult puzzle. However, as Lily looked at the storm clouds, she realized that it made her canvas more interesting and helped her become stronger. The canvas began to fill with different hues - green for new friendships, red for moments of courage, and purple. for colors when Lily tried something new. Each stroke told a story of growth and learning. As she continued to paint, Lily noticed how successes and failures danced across her canvas. The bright spots of victory made the failures less bleak, and the challenges added to her overall masterpiece. Finally, Lily stepped back to admire her canvas. It was a beautiful representation of her growth, full of bright colors and unique brush strokes. She realized that every success and failure contributed to her becoming the amazing artist she has become. Smiling with satisfaction, Lily decided that her magic paintbrush was not just for her canvas, it was a tool that brought joy and inspiration to everyone. . . In creativity Little did he know that his story would inspire others to pick up their own brushes and create unique masterpieces of growth in the city of Creativia. And so the adventures of the magic brush continued, bringing color and life to the canvas of every inhabitant of this enchanting city.

## TRY THESE!

**1. What is the name of the artist in the story?**

    a. Rose

    b. Lily

    c. Daisy

    d. Violet

**2. What kind of brush did Lily have?**

    a. Normal brush

    b. Enchanted brush

    c. Magic brush

    d. Colorful brush

**3. What could Lily's magic brush do?**

    a. Talk

    b. Bring drawings to life

    c. Fly

    d. Change colors

**4. What did Lily decide to paint with her magic brush?**

    a. A landscape

    b. A self-portrait

    c. A canvas representing her growth

    d. A cityscape

**5. What did the bright yellow paint symbolize on Lily's canvas?**

    a. Storm clouds

    b. Moments of courage

    c. Sunny days of happiness

    d. Failures

**6. What added a warm and happy glow to Lily's canvas?**

    a. Green paint

    b. Purple paint

    c. The successful bicycle ride

    d. Storm clouds

**7. What color did Lily choose to represent the challenges she faced?**

    a. Yellow

    b. Blue

    c. Green

    d. Red

**8. What did Lily paint to represent failure on her canvas?**

    a. Storm clouds

    b. A puzzle

    c. Moments of courage

    d. New friendships

**9. How did Lily feel about the storm clouds on her canvas?**

    a. Disappointed

    b. Happy

    c. Proud

    d. Surprised

**10. What did Lily paint green on her canvas?**

    a. Storm clouds

    b. Failures

    c. New friendships

    d. Moments of courage

**11. What color did red represent on Lily's canvas?**

    a. Storm clouds

    b. Failures

    c. Moments of courage

    d. New friendships

**12. What color did Lily choose for moments of courage on her canvas?**

    a. Green

    b. Red

    c. Blue

    d. Purple

**13. What did Lily paint purple on her canvas?**

    a. Storm clouds

    b. Failures

    c. Moments of courage

    d. New friendships

**14. What did each stroke on Lily's canvas represent?**

    a. Success

    b. Growth and learning

    c. Failure

    d. Challenges

**15. What did Lily notice as she continued to paint her canvas?**

    a. The canvas becoming dull

    b. Successes and failures dancing across the canvas

    c. The magic brush losing its power

    d. Challenges overshadowing victories

16. **How did Lily feel about the successes and failures on her canvas?**

    a. Disheartened

    b. Indifferent

    c. Proud

    d. Confused

17. **What did Lily's canvas become as she painted?**

    a. A dull representation

    b. A chaotic mix of colors

    c. A beautiful representation of her growth

    d. A blank slate

18. **What did Lily realize about her canvas in the end?**

    a. It lacked color

    b. It was not interesting

    c. It represented her growth

    d. It needed more challenges

19. **How did Lily feel when she stepped back to admire her canvas?**

    a. Confused

    b. Disappointed

    c. Satisfied

    d. Anxious

20. **What did Lily decide about her magic paintbrush in the end?**

    a. It was only for her canvas

    b. It brought joy and inspiration to everyone

    c. It needed more magic

    d. It lost its power

21. **What did Lily's story inspire others to do in the city of Creativia?**

    a. Stop painting

    b. Give up on their dreams

c. Pick up their own brushes and create unique masterpieces of growth

d. Leave the city

## 22. What did Lily's magic brush bring to the canvas of every inhabitant in Creativia?

a. Storm clouds

b. Challenges

c. Color and life

d. Failures

## 23. What city did Lily live in?

a. Rainbow City

b. Creativia

c. Enchanted City

d. Colorful City

## 24. What was Lily's studio full of?

a. Black and white colors

b. Rainbow colors

c. Only blue colors

d. Gray colors

## 25. What did Lily's canvas represent according to the story?

a. A random painting

b. Her failures

c. A journey of growing up

d. A cityscape

## 26. What was the color chosen for challenges in the story?

a. Yellow

b. Blue

c. Green

d. Red

27. **How did Lily feel about the storm clouds on her canvas in the end?**

    a. Disappointed

    b. Happy

    c. Proud

    d. Surprised

28. **What did Lily's canvas become as she continued to paint?**

    a. A chaotic mix of colors

    b. A blank slate

    c. A beautiful representation of her growth

    d. A dull representation

29. **What did Lily's canvas symbolize in the story?**

    a. Failures

    b. Challenges

    c. Growth and learning

    d. Successes

30. **What did Lily decide about her magic paintbrush in the end?**

    a. It was only for her canvas

    b. It brought joy and inspiration to everyone

    c. It needed more magic

    d. It lost its power

# CHAPTER 3
# PALETTE OF RELATIONSHIPS

Once upon a time, in the quaint town of Harmonyville, there lived a diverse community of individuals, each weaving their unique thread into the intricate tapestry of life. In this idyllic setting, relationships unfolded like the myriad colors on an artist's palette, creating a rich and vibrant canvas of human connections.

The protagonist of our tale is Emily, a young woman with a heart full of kindness and a spirit brimming with curiosity. Emily was a painter, and her studio was a sanctuary where canvases came to life under the strokes of her brush. However, it wasn't just her artwork that flourished; it was the relationships she cultivated that added depth and meaning to her existence.

Emily's family, a mosaic of personalities, played a central role in shaping her worldview. Her parents, Martha and Henry, were the pillars of love and support that anchored her during life's storms. Martha's warm embrace and Henry's wise counsel formed the foundation upon which Emily built her life. Together, they created a home filled with laughter, shared dreams, and the comforting aroma of Martha's homemade apple pie.

The town of Harmonyville was a close-knit community where neighbors weren't just acquaintances but an extended family. The Johnsons next door, an elderly couple with a lifetime of stories etched in their wrinkles, became surrogate grandparents to Emily. Mrs. Johnson's garden, a kaleidoscope of colors, became a playground for Emily's imagination, and Mr. Johnson's tales of bygone eras fueled her love for history.

Emily's best friend, Sarah, was a constant companion on the journey of life. Their friendship was a testament to the palette of relationships, blending hues of trust, shared secrets, and the joy of shared adventures. Sarah's infectious enthusiasm and unwavering loyalty provided Emily with a canvas of memories that would endure the tests of time.

As Emily navigated through the twists and turns of adolescence, she encountered the brushstrokes of love. Enter James, a kindred spirit who shared Emily's passion for art and saw the world through the same kaleidoscopic lens. Their love story unfolded like a masterpiece, each moment a stroke of affection and understanding that added depth to their canvas of togetherness.

However, the palette of relationships wasn't limited to familial and romantic ties; it extended to the broader community. Emily, with her innate desire to make a difference, volunteered at the local community center. There, she met a diverse array of individuals, each contributing their unique color to the collective canvas of humanity. From the wise elderly to the energetic youth, the community center became a melting pot of stories, a testament to the beauty that emerges when people from different walks of life come together.

As Emily continued to paint the canvas of her life, she faced challenges that tested the resilience of her relationships. The loss of a loved one cast shadows on the once vibrant palette, but it also brought forth the hues of empathy, compassion, and the enduring strength of unity. Together with her family, friends, and the broader community, Emily navigated through grief, adding a poignant layer to her evolving tapestry.

Friendships evolved, and new characters entered Emily's narrative. The shy artist from the neighboring town, the boisterous chef who owned the local diner, and the mysterious storyteller who frequented the town square—all left their mark on Emily's canvas. Each encounter, whether brief or enduring, contributed to the ever-expanding palette of relationships that defined her life.

In the tapestry of Harmonyville, forgiveness became a prominent color. Misunderstandings, disagreements, and the inevitable conflicts that arise in any community became opportunities for growth. Forgiveness wasn't just an act; it was a transformative brushstroke that mended frayed edges and added resilience to the intricate patterns of connection.

Through the seasons of life, Emily's relationships continued to evolve. The bonds with her parents deepened into a profound understanding of the sacrifices and love that defined familial ties. Her friendship with Sarah weathered the storms of change, emerging stronger with shared laughter and tears. The love between Emily and James blossomed into a partnership that faced challenges hand in hand, their commitment an enduring masterpiece on the canvas of commitment.

As Emily embraced the joys of motherhood, the palette of relationships expanded to include the newest additions to her family. The laughter of children, the advice of experienced parents, and the collective wisdom of generations blended into a symphony of colors, creating a harmonious melody that resonated through the town.

In the twilight of her years, Emily sat in her studio, surrounded by the artwork that mirrored the journey of a lifetime. The canvas was a testament to the ebb and flow of relationships—the moments of joy, the challenges that added depth, and the enduring beauty of connections forged in the crucible of shared experiences.

Harmonyville, with its diverse cast of characters, mirrored the universal truth that relationships form the very fabric of our existence. Each person, a brushstroke on the canvas of life, contributed to a collective masterpiece that transcended individual stories. The palette of relationships, with its myriad colors, revealed the richness of human connection—the tapestry of shared joys, sorrows, and the enduring beauty that emerged when hearts intertwined in the grand symphony of existence.

And so, in the heart of Harmonyville, where the brushstrokes of life painted a canvas of relationships, Emily's story became a timeless ode to the intricate dance of human connections—a testament to the enduring power of love, understanding, and the shared journey that weaves us all into the tapestry of life.

## TRY THESE!

**1. What town is the setting for the story?**

    a. Serenity Springs

    b. Harmonyville

    c. Tranquil Meadows

    d. Peaceful Haven

**2. What is Emily's profession?**

    a. Chef

    b. Painter

    c. Storyteller

    d. Musician

**3. What is Emily's studio described as?**

    a. A sanctuary for writers

    b. A kitchen filled with aromas

    c. A canvas of memories

    d. A sanctuary where canvases come to life under the strokes of her brush

**4. Who are Emily's parents?**

a. John and Susan

b. Martha and Henry

c. Robert and Eleanor

d. David and Catherine

**5. What does Martha make that fills their home with a comforting aroma?**

a. Apple pie

b. Chocolate cake

c. Fresh bread

d. Roast chicken

**6. Who are the Johnsons in Emily's life?**

a. Friends from school

b. Colleagues from work

c. Surrogate grandparents

d. Distant relatives

**7. What does Mrs. Johnson's garden become for Emily?**

a. A playground for imagination

b. A source of conflict

c. A place to practice painting

d. A vegetable garden

**8. What does Mr. Johnson's tales fuel Emily's love for?**

a. Cooking

b. Music

c. History

d. Gardening

**9. Who is Emily's best friend in the story?**

a. Lily

b. Sarah

c. James

d. Thomas

10. **What qualities are mentioned about Sarah's friendship with Emily?**

    a. Trust, shared secrets, and the joy of shared adventures

    b. Competition, jealousy, and rivalry

    c. Indifference, secrecy, and isolation

    d. Betrayal, lies, and conflicts

11. **What does Emily encounter in adolescence that adds depth to her life?**

    a. Challenges

    b. Successes

    c. Loss of family

    d. Love affairs

12. **Who is James in the story?**

    a. A chef

    b. A musician

    c. A painter

    d. A kindred spirit who shares Emily's passion for art

13. **How is James described in the story?**

    a. Boisterous and energetic

    b. Shy and reserved

    c. Mysterious and elusive

    d. Kindred spirit who shares Emily's passion for art

14. **What does Emily volunteer for in the broader community?**

    a. Local library

    b. Animal shelter

    c. Community center

    d. Art gallery

15. **What does the community center become for Emily?**

    a. A place to meet friends

    b. A hub for artistic endeavors

    c. A melting pot of stories

    d. A sports club

**16. What adds a poignant layer to Emily's tapestry in the story?**

    a. Birth of a child

    b. Loss of a loved one

    c. Career success

    d. Romantic relationship

**17. How does Emily navigate through grief in the story?**

    a. By isolating herself from others

    b. By seeking professional help

    c. By turning to her family, friends, and the community

    d. By avoiding her emotions

**18. What does forgiveness become in the tapestry of relationships?**

    a. A burden

    b. A weakness

    c. A transformative brushstroke

    d. An unnecessary gesture

**19. How do friendships evolve in Emily's life in the story?**

    a. They remain stagnant

    b. They fade away

    c. They deepen and endure

    d. They become irrelevant

**20. What do new characters bring to Emily's canvas in the story?**

    a. Conflict and rivalry

    b. Joy and laughter

    c. Grief and sorrow

    d. A sense of isolation

**21. What does the shy artist contribute to Emily's life?**

    a. A source of conflict

    b. A sense of isolation

    c. A new perspective and color to her canvas

    d. A competition in art

22. **What becomes a prominent color in the tapestry of Harmonyville?**

   a. Jealousy

   b. Forgiveness

   c. Grief

   d. Indifference

23. **How does Emily's relationship with her parents evolve through the seasons of life?**

   a. It remains stagnant

   b. It becomes strained

   c. It deepens into a profound understanding

   d. It fades away

24. **What is the enduring masterpiece on the canvas of commitment in Emily's life?**

   a. Friendship with Sarah

   b. Relationship with James

   c. Career success

   d. Volunteering at the community center

25. **What expands the palette of relationships as Emily embraces motherhood?**

   a. Loss of a loved one

   b. Laughter of children

   c. Conflicts with friends

   d. Isolation from the community

26. **In the twilight of her years, where does Emily sit surrounded by the artwork?**

   a. In her bedroom

   b. In her kitchen

   c. In her garden

   d. In her studio

**27. What does the canvas represent according to the story?**

    a. A blank slate

    b. A representation of Emily's art

    c. A journey of life and relationships

    d. A source of conflict

**28. What does Harmonyville mirror in the story?**

    a. The chaos of urban life

    b. The diversity of relationships

    c. The isolation of small towns

    d. The insignificance of human connections

**29. What is each person in the story described as?**

    a. A blank slate

    b. A brushstroke on the canvas of life

    c. An irrelevant character

    d. A burden in Emily's life

**30. What does the palette of relationships reveal in the story?**

    a. The insignificance of human connection

    b. The richness of human connection

    c. The isolation of small towns

    d. The chaos of urban life

# CHAPTER 4
# SHADOWS AND LIGHT

In the quaint town of Lumina, where shadows danced playfully with light, there lived a young woman named Amelia. Lumina was a unique place where the residents cherished the interplay of shadows and light, recognizing that both were essential in the grand tapestry of life.

Amelia was an artist with a keen appreciation for the nuances of existence. Her small studio, nestled between two charming houses, was a haven of creativity. The walls were adorned with her masterpieces, each one capturing the delicate balance of shadows and light in the world around her.

One day, as the sun dipped below the horizon, casting long shadows across Lumina, Amelia felt an undeniable urge to explore the deeper meaning behind the interplay of shadows and light. She decided to embark on a journey, not just within her town but also within herself, seeking to unravel the mysteries that these contrasting elements held.

Amelia began her exploration by wandering through the cobbled streets of Lumina. The warm glow of street lamps cast enchanting shadows on the pavement, creating a mesmerizing dance of dark and light. As she strolled, she encountered the townsfolk going about their evening routines.

In Lumina, people embraced both the shadows and the light. They understood that life was a delicate dance, a symphony of contrasts that painted the canvas of their shared existence. Amelia observed how the soft glow of windows spilled onto the streets, inviting shadows to weave intricate patterns on the facades of buildings.

Her journey took her to the heart of Lumina, where the town square bustled with activity. A lively market was in full swing, with vendors selling their wares beneath colorful awnings. The play of shadows on the vibrant stalls added an extra layer of charm to the scene.

Amelia's attention was drawn to a street performer, a mime who skillfully manipulated shadows to tell stories. The children gathered around, captivated by the tales woven by the interplay of light and darkness. It was a beautiful reminder that even in the simplest gestures, shadows and light collaborated to create magic.

As Amelia continued her journey, she entered Lumina's lush park. The moon cast a gentle glow, and the trees created intricate patterns of shadows on the ground. She found a secluded bench and marveled at the peaceful coexistence of shadows and light in nature.

Inspired by the beauty around her, Amelia returned to her studio with a newfound sense of purpose. She felt compelled to translate her experiences into her art. Night after night, she worked tirelessly on a series of paintings that sought to capture the essence of Lumina's dance between shadows and light.

One of her most compelling pieces depicted a solitary figure, bathed in the soft glow of a streetlamp, surrounded by elongated shadows that seemed to reach out in every direction. The painting spoke of solitude and contemplation, highlighting the beauty found in moments of quiet reflection.

Another artwork portrayed the town square during the market day, with vendors bustling beneath a canopy of vibrant umbrellas. The play of shadows and light on the cheerful faces of the townsfolk conveyed the joy of community and shared experiences.

As Amelia continued to create, her art became a mirror reflecting the intricate tapestry of life in Lumina. Each stroke of her brush was a testament to the understanding that shadows and light were not opposing forces but rather complementary aspects of a greater whole.

Word of Amelia's art spread throughout Lumina, and soon, her studio became a gathering place for those who sought to explore the deeper meanings of life. The townsfolk engaged in conversations about their own experiences with shadows and light, sharing stories that ranged from moments of adversity to triumphs of resilience.

One evening, as Lumina was bathed in the warm hues of sunset, Amelia decided to host an exhibition featuring her collection. The entire town turned out to witness the unveiling of her creations. The walls of her studio became a gallery of life, where the interplay of shadows and light conveyed the rich tapestry of human existence.

The first painting on display depicted a sunrise over Lumina, casting long shadows that stretched across the landscape. It symbolized new beginnings and the infinite possibilities that each day brought. The townsfolk marveled at the details, feeling a collective sense of hope and renewal.

Amelia's artwork continued to unfold, telling stories of love, loss, resilience, and the myriad emotions that colored the human experience. The exhibition became a celebration of the town's shared journey, a visual symphony that resonated with the hearts of those who beheld it.

In the midst of the exhibition, Amelia noticed an elderly woman standing before a painting that depicted the moonlit park. The woman's eyes glistened with tears as she recounted a cherished memory of strolls in the park with her late husband. The shadows cast by the trees became a poignant reminder of the enduring light of love, even in the face of loss.

As the night descended upon Lumina, the exhibition took on a magical quality. The paintings seemed to come alive, their stories whispered in hushed tones that resonated with the collective soul of the town. Shadows and light played together, creating an atmosphere of enchantment and unity.

Amelia's journey of exploration had not only enriched her own understanding of shadows and light but had also woven a tapestry that connected the hearts of Lumina's residents. The town, once illuminated by the physical light of street lamps and the metaphorical light of shared experiences, became a beacon of inspiration for all who visited.

In the days that followed, Lumina continued to embrace the dance of shadows and light. The townsfolk found solace in the understanding that both elements were integral to their collective narrative. Amelia's studio remained a hub of creativity, a place where stories were shared, and new artworks were born, each one adding to the rich tapestry of Lumina's existence.

And so, in the colorful town of Lumina, where shadows and light coexisted in perfect harmony, the canvas of life continued to unfold, revealing the intricate beauty that could only be discovered through the interplay of contrasting elements.

## TRY THESE!

### 1. What is the name of the town where Amelia lives?

 a. Radiantville

 b. Luminosity

 c. Lumina

 d. Shadowville

2. **What does Lumina's unique atmosphere involve?**

    a. A clash of shadows and light

    b. An absence of shadows

    c. Monochromatic surroundings

    d. A dominance of darkness

3. **Where is Amelia's small studio located?**

    a. Between two mountains

    b. Nestled between two oceans

    c. Between two charming houses

    d. In the heart of Lumina's park

4. **What does Amelia's art primarily focus on capturing?**

    a. Monotony

    b. The interplay of shadows and light

    c. Darkness alone

    d. Vibrant colors only

5. **What does the town of Lumina cherish, according to the story?**

    a. The absence of shadows

    b. The interplay of shadows and light

    c. Darkness alone

    d. Monotony

6. **When did Amelia feel the urge to explore the meaning behind shadows and light?**

    a. Sunrise

    b. Sunset

    c. Midnight

    d. Noon

7. **What was Lumina like as the sun dipped below the horizon?**

    a. Dark and gloomy

    b. Bathed in warm hues

    c. Radiant with artificial light

    d. Absence of any light

8. **What did Amelia decide to explore during her journey?**

   a. The mysteries of shadows only

   b. The mysteries of light only

   c. The deeper meaning behind the interplay of shadows and light

   d. The history of Lumina

9. **What did Amelia's studio become for the townsfolk?**

   a. A hub of darkness

   b. A gathering place for creative discussions

   c. A place devoid of any art

   d. A place only for Amelia's personal use

10. **What did Lumina's residents understand about life?**

    a. Life as a monochromatic existence

    b. Life as a symphony of contrasts

    c. Life as a shadowless journey

    d. Life as a journey dominated by darkness

11. **How did Lumina's townsfolk embrace shadows and light?**

    a. By avoiding both

    b. By understanding their delicate dance

    c. By banishing shadows

    d. By focusing only on shadows

12. **What did Amelia observe on the facades of buildings as she strolled through Lumina?**

    a. Plain walls with no patterns

    b. Intricate patterns woven by shadows and light

    c. Colorful graffiti

    d. Absence of any architectural details

13. **What added an extra layer of charm to Lumina's market square?**

    a. Complete darkness

    b. The absence of any activity

    c. The play of shadows on the vibrant stalls

    d. A monotonous atmosphere

**14. What caught Amelia's attention in the town square?**

    a. A deserted square

    b. A lively market

    c. Silent vendors

    d. An absence of colors

**15. What did the street performer manipulate to tell stories?**

    a. Shadows only

    b. Light only

    c. Shadows and light

    d. Colors

**16. What did the mime use to captivate the children in Lumina?**

    a. Shadows only

    b. Light only

    c. Both shadows and light

    d. Colors

**17. How did Amelia feel about the mime's performance?**

    a. Indifferent

    b. Enchanted

    c. Disinterested

    d. Confused

**18. Where did Amelia find a secluded bench to marvel at the interplay of shadows and light in nature?**

    a. In her studio

    b. In Lumina's park

    c. In the market square

    d. In a dark alley

**19. What did Amelia decide to do upon returning to her studio?**

    a. Abandon her art

    b. Translate her experiences into her art

    c. Close her studio

    d. Switch to painting only in black and white

20. **What did one of Amelia's compelling pieces depict?**

   a. A bustling market square

   b. A solitary figure bathed in a streetlamp's glow

   c. A monochromatic landscape

   d. A completely dark scene

21. **What did the painting of a solitary figure symbolize?**

   a. Joy and celebration

   b. Solitude and contemplation

   c. Darkness and despair

   d. A lack of any emotion

22. **What did another artwork portray in Lumina's town square?**

   a. An empty square

   b. Vendors selling wares beneath colorful umbrellas

   c. A dark and gloomy atmosphere

   d. An absence of any activity

23. **How did Amelia's art become a mirror reflecting life in Lumina?**

   a. By focusing only on darkness

   b. By avoiding colors

   c. By capturing the delicate balance of shadows and light

   d. By painting only in black and white

24. **What did Amelia's studio become for those seeking deeper meanings of life?**

   a. A hub of darkness

   b. A place for silence

   c. A gathering place for creative discussions

   d. A place devoid of any art

25. **What did Amelia decide to host as Lumina was bathed in the warm hues of sunset?**

   a. A silent gathering

   b. A music concert

c. An exhibition featuring her collection

d. A dance performance

## 26. What did the first painting on display symbolize?

a. Endings and closures

b. New beginnings and infinite possibilities

c. Darkness and despair

d. Monotonous existence

## 27. What did the exhibition become a celebration of?

a. Darkness alone

b. The town's shared journey

c. The absence of shadows

d. A monochromatic existence

## 28. What did the moonlit park painting evoke in an elderly woman?

a. Fear

b. Joy

c. Nostalgia and tears

d. A sense of peace

## 29. How did the exhibition take on a magical quality as night descended upon Lumina?

a. By becoming darker

b. By the paintings coming to life

c. By losing its charm

d. By turning monochromatic

## 30. What did Amelia's journey of exploration enrich?

a. Her understanding of shadows only

b. Her understanding of light only

c. Her understanding of shadows and light as complementary aspects

d. Her understanding of the absence of shadows and light

# CHAPTER 5
# ART OF SELF DISCOVERY

In the heart of a quaint town, nestled between rolling hills and the soft whispers of rustling leaves, lived a woman named Amelia. She was an artist with a soul adorned with vibrant dreams and an insatiable curiosity for the mysteries of life. Amelia's world was filled with canvases, paintbrushes, and the intoxicating scent of creativity that danced through her studio like a lively muse.

Amelia's art was not just about colors and strokes; it was a journey into the realms of self-discovery. Every canvas she touched became a mirror reflecting the hues of her inner landscape. Her studio, with its scattered brushes and splattered palettes, was a sanctuary where she embarked on a pilgrimage of understanding the depths of her being.

Her artistic odyssey began with a blank canvas, much like the untrodden paths of self-discovery. The canvas, an open invitation to her soul, awaited the first stroke that would set the tone for the masterpiece yet to unfold. Amelia, armed with a spectrum of emotions and the bravery to confront her vulnerabilities, dipped her brush into the palette of life.

The initial strokes were tentative, mirroring the cautious steps one takes when venturing into the unknown corridors of self. Amelia painted swirls of uncertainty, blending them with streaks of courage as she navigated the labyrinth of her emotions. Each dab of color held a whisper of introspection, a dialogue with the silent chambers of her heart.

As the painting evolved, Amelia found herself entwined in the dance of light and shadow, much like the intricate play of strengths and weaknesses within. The canvas bore witness to the moments of joy that burst forth like sunbeams and the shadows that cast their gentle reminders of life's inevitable struggles.

Her journey of self-discovery delved deeper, reaching the reservoirs of memory and experience. Amelia painted landscapes reminiscent of her childhood, with the innocence of laughter and the fragrance of wildflowers that once adorned her grandmother's garden. Through the strokes, she rekindled forgotten tales and rediscovered the roots that shaped her existence.

Yet, the canvas also bore witness to the storms she weathered – the tumultuous seas of heartbreak, the fierce winds of disappointment, and the thunderous clashes of shattered dreams. In those moments, Amelia's art became a cathartic release, a sanctuary where pain transformed into resilience, and wounds into brushstrokes of healing.

Amelia's hands moved gracefully, weaving the tapestry of her life on the canvas. She painted the pages of her journal with swirls of love, loss, and the ceaseless quest for meaning. Each stroke was an affirmation of her identity, a declaration that every scar, every triumph, was an integral part of the masterpiece she was becoming.

The art of self-discovery led Amelia to explore the vast landscapes of her passions. Through the vibrant strokes of her brush, she embraced the symphony of music that echoed in her soul, the poetry that whispered in the wind, and the dance of movement that embodied the rhythm of her existence. The canvas transformed into a kaleidoscope of her passions, a celebration of the diverse hues that painted the mural of her life.

With each passing stroke, Amelia unearthed the layers of her authenticity. She painted the masks she wore, the roles she played, and the expectations she carried. The canvas became a mirror reflecting the woman behind the veils, peeling away the layers until she stood in the raw beauty of her truth.

Amelia's self-discovery was not without its share of introspective challenges. The canvas witnessed the moments of self-doubt, the shadows of insecurities, and the questions that echoed in the corridors of her mind. Yet, with each stroke, she transformed those doubts into affirmations, those shadows into stepping stones, and those questions into a journey of continuous exploration.

As the canvas neared completion, Amelia stood before a masterpiece that mirrored the kaleidoscope of her life. The vibrant colors of joy, the muted tones of sorrow, and the contrasting shades of strength and vulnerability blended seamlessly into a reflection of a woman who had embraced the art of self-discovery.

With a profound sense of fulfillment, Amelia realized that the canvas was not just a testament to her journey but an invitation for others to embark on their odyssey of self-discovery. Her studio became a haven where kindred souls sought solace in the strokes of a paintbrush, where whispers of vulnerability echoed in the laughter and tears shared within those sacred walls.

In the quietude of her studio, as the sun dipped below the horizon and painted the sky with hues of twilight, Amelia stood as a testament to the transformative power of self-discovery. Her art was not confined to canvases; it echoed in the lives she touched, the stories she inspired, and the authenticity she radiated.

And so, in the heart of that quaint town, where the rolling hills cradled the dreams of its inhabitants, Amelia's studio stood as a testament to the art of self-discovery. It was a sanctuary where the canvases breathed with the essence of life, and each stroke whispered the timeless truth that, in the dance of colors, we uncover the masterpiece of our own existence.

## TRY THESE!

**1. What is the setting of the story?**

    a. A bustling city

    b. A quaint town

    c. A coastal village

    d. A mountain retreat

**2. What is Amelia's profession?**

    a. Chef

    b. Musician

    c. Artist

    d. Scientist

**3. What is the initial state of the canvas at the beginning of the story?**

    a. Filled with vibrant colors

    b. Blank and waiting

    c. Covered in sketches

    d. Displaying a finished masterpiece

**4. What is the metaphorical purpose of the canvas in the story?**

   a. A mirror reflecting the town's beauty

   b. A representation of the protagonist's inner journey

   c. A map of the protagonist's travels

   d. A showcase of different art styles

**5. What does Amelia's studio smell like?**

   a. Coffee

   b. Freshly baked bread

   c. Creativity

   d. Perfume

**6. What is Amelia's journey compared to in the story?**

   a. A labyrinth

   b. A sprint

   c. A marathon

   d. A puzzle

**7. What does the first stroke on the canvas represent for Amelia?**

   a. Uncertainty

   b. Boldness

   c. Achievement

   d. Nostalgia

**8. What emotions are reflected in the tentative strokes of Amelia's brush?**

   a. Joy and happiness

   b. Uncertainty and courage

   c. Sadness and disappointment

   d. Excitement and enthusiasm

**9. What does the canvas mirror as it evolves in the story?**

   a. Town events

   b. Protagonist's inner landscape

   c. Changing seasons

   d. Historical landmarks

10. **What is the labyrinth within which Amelia navigates in the story?**

    a. Her studio

    b. The canvas

    c. The town

    d. Her dreams

11. **What do the swirls of uncertainty symbolize in the story?**

    a. Past achievements

    b. Inner courage

    c. Future challenges

    d. Present achievements

12. **What does the canvas witness during Amelia's journey of self-discovery?**

    a. Town events

    b. Changes in the weather

    c. Personal moments and emotions

    d. Historical events

13. **What does Amelia's journey delve deeper into in the story?**

    a. Historical events

    b. The town's architecture

    c. Her childhood memories and experiences

    d. Changing seasons

14. **What transforms pain into resilience in Amelia's art?**

    a. Challenges

    b. Past achievements

    c. Inner courage

    d. Successes

15. **What does the canvas become during moments of cathartic release?**

    a. A labyrinth

    b. A sanctuary

c. A cityscape

d. A puzzle

**16. What does Amelia paint to represent her childhood memories?**

a. Swirls of uncertainty

b. Storm clouds

c. Innocence of laughter and wildflowers

d. Moments of courage

**17. What does the canvas bear witness to during Amelia's journey?**

a. Challenges and triumphs

b. Town events only

c. Historical landmarks only

d. Changing seasons only

**18. How does Amelia transform doubts and insecurities in the story?**

a. By hiding them

b. By affirmations and stepping stones

c. By ignoring them

d. By emphasizing them

**19. What does Amelia unveil with each passing stroke on the canvas?**

a. Her studio

b. Layers of her authenticity

c. The town's history

d. Changing seasons

**20. What does Amelia's studio become for kindred souls in the story?**

a. A cafe

b. A library

c. A sanctuary

d. A school

21. **What is the canvas an invitation for others to embark on in the story?**

    a. A physical journey

    b. A journey of self-discovery

    c. A town event

    d. A historical journey

22. **What does Amelia's art bring to the lives of those in the town?**

    a. Storm clouds

    b. Challenges

    c. Color and life

    d. Failures

23. **What stands as a testament to the transformative power of self-discovery in the story?**

    a. Amelia's brushes

    b. Amelia's art

    c. The town's architecture

    d. Changing seasons

24. **What metaphor is used for Amelia's hands in the story?**

    a. Trees

    b. Leaves

    c. Swirls

    d. Waves

25. **What does Amelia stand as in the story?**

    a. A tourist

    b. A testament

    c. A painter

    d. A musician

26. **What does the canvas echo in the lives of those touched by Amelia's art?**

    a. Changing seasons

    b. Challenges

c. Stories inspired and authenticity radiated

d. Town events

## 27. What colors are reflected in the completed canvas of Amelia's life?

a. Black and white

b. Joy and happiness

c. Chaos and confusion

d. Success and failure

## 28. What is the canvas an invitation for others to embark on in the story?

a. A physical journey

b. A journey of self-discovery

c. A town event

d. A historical journey

## 29. What does Amelia's studio symbolize in the story?

a. A cafe

b. A library

c. A sanctuary

d. A school

## 30. What is the timeless truth revealed in the story?

a. In the dance of colors, we uncover the masterpiece of our own existence

b. In the dance of challenges, we uncover the masterpiece of our own existence

c. In the dance of changing seasons, we uncover the masterpiece of our own existence

d. In the dance of town events, we uncover the masterpiece of our own existence

# CHAPTER 6
# SEASONS OF CHANGE

Once upon a time, in a quaint town nestled between rolling hills and lush meadows, there lived a young woman named Emily. The town, known for its picturesque landscapes and vibrant community, was a haven for those seeking the simple beauty of life.

Emily's story began in the vibrant burst of spring, where the town bloomed with an array of colors and fragrances. She was a dreamer, with an insatiable curiosity that mirrored the blossoming flowers around her. Emily's days were filled with exploring the meadows, chasing butterflies, and finding joy in the smallest wonders.

As the town transitioned into the warmth of summer, Emily found herself on the cusp of adolescence. The air was filled with the sounds of laughter and the scent of freshly mown grass. Summer brought with it a sense of freedom, and Emily embraced it wholeheartedly. She spent long, lazy days with her friends, sharing stories and building memories that would linger in her heart for years to come.

The arrival of autumn marked a shift in the town's atmosphere. The vibrant greens transformed into a tapestry of red, orange, and gold. Emily, now a young woman, navigated the season of change in her own life. She embarked on a journey of self-discovery, trying to understand the ever-evolving canvas of her emotions and aspirations. Autumn's crisp air whispered secrets of transformation, and Emily embraced the challenge of shedding old leaves to make way for new growth.

As winter descended upon the town, blanketing it in a serene hush, Emily faced the quiet introspection that the season brought. The world around her seemed to slow down, mirroring the stillness within. Winter was a time for reflection, a season that encouraged her to delve into the depths of her soul. Emily found solace in the simplicity of a snow-covered landscape and the warmth of a crackling fireplace.

With the advent of another spring, Emily emerged from the cocoon of winter, her spirit renewed and invigorated. The cycle of seasons mirrored the cycles of her life, each phase contributing to her growth and resilience. Spring brought with it a sense of rebirth, and Emily embraced the opportunity to start anew.

Years passed, and Emily's story continued to unfold with the rhythm of the changing seasons. Through the highs and lows, the laughter and tears, she discovered the profound beauty of life's transitions. Each season, with its unique characteristics, taught her valuable lessons about resilience, gratitude, and the inevitability of change.

In the warmth of summer, Emily experienced the intoxicating dance of love. Romance blossomed like the flowers in the meadows, and she found a kindred spirit with whom to share the journey. Together, they explored the vibrant landscapes of the town, creating a mosaic of shared memories that became the foundation of a lifelong bond.

As autumn approached once again, Emily faced the challenges of adulthood. Responsibilities and decisions weighed on her shoulders like the falling leaves, but she navigated the complexities with grace and determination. The tapestry of her life became richer with experiences, and she learned to appreciate the beauty in the impermanence of each moment.

Winter returned, bringing with it moments of quiet contemplation. Emily, now a seasoned traveler through the seasons of life, found joy in the simple pleasures of connection and reflection. The snow-covered town became a canvas for memories, each snowflake a reminder of the intricate details that made her journey uniquely hers.

With the emergence of yet another spring, Emily stood at the crossroads of her story. The town, familiar yet ever-changing, mirrored the ebb and flow of her own existence. As the seasons continued their eternal dance, Emily embraced the uncertainty of the future with a heart full of gratitude for the lessons each season had bestowed upon her.

In the twilight of her years, surrounded by the warmth of a summer sunset, Emily reflected on a life well-lived. The seasons had been her greatest teachers, guiding her through the myriad experiences that shaped her into the person she had become. Through the vibrant hues of spring, the carefree days of summer, the contemplative moments of autumn, and the serene stillness of winter, Emily had discovered the true essence of existence.

As the final season of her life approached, Emily welcomed it with the same acceptance and resilience that had defined her journey. The cycle of seasons continued, an eternal reminder that life, like nature itself, is a beautiful and ever-changing tapestry. And so, in the quiet embrace of the town she had called home, Emily's story reached its conclusion, leaving behind a legacy woven into the fabric of the changing seasons.

**TRY THESE!**

**1. What is the protagonist's name in the story?**

    a. Emily

    b. Lily

    c. Rose

    d. Daisy

**2. In which season did Emily's story begin?**

    a. Summer

    b. Autumn

    c. Spring

    d. Winter

**3. What was special about Emily's brush?**

    a. It could fly

    b. It talked

    c. It changed colors

    d. It brought drawings to life

**4. What did the bright yellow paint symbolize on Lily's canvas?**

    a. Moments of courage

    b. Sunny days of happiness

    c. Failures

    d. Storm clouds

**5. What color did Lily choose to represent the challenges she faced?**

    a. Yellow

    b. Blue

    c. Green

    d. Red

**6. What did Emily embrace during the warmth of summer?**

    a. Winter activities

    b. Freedom and exploration

    c. Self-discovery

    d. Quiet introspection

7. **What did Emily find solace in during winter?**

    a. Blossoming flowers

    b. Crisp autumn air

    c. The warmth of a fireplace

    d. Chasing butterflies

8. **What season marked a shift in the town's atmosphere in Emily's story?**

    a. Summer

    b. Autumn

    c. Spring

    d. Winter

9. **What did Lily realize about her canvas as she continued to paint?**

    a. It became dull

    b. Challenges overshadowed victories

    c. Successes and failures danced across it

    d. It needed more colors

10. **What did Lily decide about her magic paintbrush in the end?**

    a. It was only for her canvas

    b. It brought joy and inspiration to everyone

    c. It needed more magic

    d. It lost its power

11. **How did Emily feel about the successes and failures on her canvas?**

    a. Disheartened

    b. Indifferent

    c. Proud

    d. Confused

12. **What did Lily's story inspire others to do in the city of Creativia?**

    a. Stop painting

    b. Give up on their dreams

c. Pick up their own brushes and create unique masterpieces of growth

d. Leave the city

## 13. What was the town known for in Emily's story?

a. Enchanting forests

b. Rolling hills

c. Quaint meadows

d. Picturesque landscapes

## 14. What did Emily face during the season of autumn?

a. Chasing butterflies

b. Blossoming flowers

c. Challenges and self-discovery

d. Quiet introspection

## 15. What was the canvas compared to in the story?

a. A magical world

b. A grand painting with characters

c. An intricate tapestry

d. A hidden treasure

## 16. What did Emily find joy in during the quiet introspection of winter?

a. Chasing butterflies

b. The simplicity of a snow-covered landscape

c. Blossoming flowers

d. Exploring meadows

## 17. What did Emily's canvas become as she painted?

a. A chaotic mix of colors

b. A blank slate

c. A beautiful representation of her growth

d. A dull representation

18. **What did Emily embrace in the warmth of summer?**

    a. Autumn's crisp air

    b. Freedom and exploration

    c. Winter's quiet introspection

    d. Chasing butterflies

19. **What color did Lily choose for moments of courage on her canvas?**

    a. Green

    b. Red

    c. Blue

    d. Purple

20. **What did the canvas represent according to the story?**

    a. A random painting

    b. Her failures

    c. A journey of growing up

    d. A cityscape

21. **What did Lily's canvas symbolize in the story?**

    a. Failures

    b. Challenges

    c. Growth and learning

    d. Successes

22. **What did Lily paint green on her canvas?**

    a. Storm clouds

    b. Failures

    c. New friendships

    d. Moments of courage

23. **What did Lily's canvas become as she continued to paint?**

    a. A chaotic mix of colors

    b. A blank slate

    c. A beautiful representation of her growth

    d. A dull representation

24. **How did Lily feel about the storm clouds on her canvas in the end?**

   a. Disappointed

   b. Happy

   c. Proud

   d. Surprised

25. **What did Lily choose to represent the challenges she faced on her canvas?**

   a. Yellow

   b. Blue

   c. Green

   d. Red

26. **What did Emily find joy in during the quiet introspection of winter?**

   a. Chasing butterflies

   b. The simplicity of a snow-covered landscape

   c. Blossoming flowers

   d. Exploring meadows

27. **What did Lily's canvas represent according to the story?**

   a. A random painting

   b. Her failures

   c. A journey of growing up

   d. A cityscape

28. **What did Emily embrace during the season of autumn?**

   a. Chasing butterflies

   b. Blossoming flowers

   c. Challenges and self-discovery

   d. Quiet introspection

29. **What did Lily find joy in during the quiet introspection of winter?**

   a. Chasing butterflies

   b. The simplicity of a snow-covered landscape

c. Blossoming flowers

d. Exploring meadows

## 30. What did Emily find solace in during winter?

a. Blossoming flowers

b. Crisp autumn air

c. The warmth of a fireplace

d. Chasing butterflies

# CHAPTER 7
# COLORS OF LEGACY

In a quaint town nestled between rolling hills and meandering rivers, there lived a community known for their vibrant traditions and close-knit bonds. The town of Harmony thrived on the colors of legacy, a rich tapestry woven by the lives of its inhabitants.

The protagonist of our story is Ella, a wise and compassionate elder who has witnessed the ebb and flow of life in Harmony for decades. Her wrinkled face told tales of laughter, sorrow, and the intricate patterns of human connection. As the sun dipped below the horizon, Ella sat on her porch, overlooking the town square, ready to share the story of Harmony's legacy.

The earliest strokes on the canvas of Harmony's legacy were painted by the founding families who settled in the town generations ago. Their determination and unity formed the base colors that still echoed through the cobblestone streets. As Ella reminisced, she spoke of the pioneer spirit that built the foundations of Harmony, each brick and beam infused with the dreams of those who sought a place to call home.

With the passage of time, the canvas gained more hues as families flourished and the town expanded. Ella described the golden fields of wheat that whispered tales of abundant harvests and shared meals. These fields, she explained, were a symbol of hard work and the sustenance of a community that relied on one another.

The color red painted a vivid picture of love and passion within Harmony's legacy. Ella spoke of the timeless romances that blossomed under the ancient oak trees, where lovers carved their initials, marking their commitment to intertwine their lives. These love stories became threads woven into the fabric of the town, creating a tapestry of enduring relationships.

As Ella continued her narrative, she delved into the green hues of growth and renewal. The town's marketplace, once a humble gathering of merchants, had burgeoned into a bustling center of commerce. The spirit of entrepreneurship thrived, and the legacy of innovation echoed through the creations of local artisans and craftsmen.

Harmony's legacy, however, was not without its shadows. Ella's eyes carried a hint of melancholy as she spoke of the challenges the town faced—the economic downturns, natural disasters, and the losses that left an indelible mark on the canvas. Yet, these challenges were not portrayed in dark, somber shades; instead, they were strokes of resilience, revealing the strength of a community that faced adversity with unwavering determination.

The canvas expanded with the introduction of education and enlightenment. Ella's eyes sparkled with pride as she described the establishment of schools and libraries, where the thirst for knowledge was quenched. The youth of Harmony embraced learning, and their intellectual pursuits added a brilliant spectrum to the colors of legacy.

Generations passed, and Ella marveled at the transformation of Harmony's legacy. The once simple town had become a mosaic of diversity, with people from different backgrounds contributing their unique hues. The town square, once a modest gathering place, now hosted festivals that celebrated the kaleidoscope of cultures present in Harmony.

Ella's narrative then shifted to the azure hues of leadership and governance. The town had witnessed the rise of wise leaders who guided Harmony through times of uncertainty. Their legacies intertwined with the very fabric of the town, leaving behind a blueprint for future leaders to follow.

The canvas of Harmony's legacy was incomplete without acknowledging the violet shades of art and expression. Ella spoke of the local artists who painted murals on walls, musicians who filled the air with melodies, and writers who penned stories that echoed the soul of the town. These creative expressions added depth and beauty to the evolving masterpiece.

As the sun dipped lower, casting a warm glow over the town square, Ella concluded her tale. The canvas of Harmony's legacy was a living testament to the interconnected lives of its inhabitants. Every stroke, every color, and every nuance represented the collective journey of a community bound by shared memories and aspirations.

In the twilight of her years, Ella passed the torch to the younger generation, urging them to carry forth the tradition of adding vibrant strokes to the canvas of Harmony's legacy. The town, she believed, had the power to inspire and leave an indelible mark on the hearts of those who called it home.

As the night settled in, the town square glowed with the warm lights of lanterns and the laughter of children playing. The legacy of Harmony continued to evolve, a living masterpiece shaped by the hands of time and the collective spirit of its people. Ella's voice, though a whisper in the wind, lingered, becoming part of the ever-expanding symphony of stories that painted the canvas of Harmony's legacy for generations to come.

**TRY THESE!**

**1. Who is the protagonist of the story?**

    a. Lily

    b. Ella

    c. Rose

    d. Violet

**2. What town is the setting for the story?**

    a. Serenity

    b. Tranquility

    c. Harmony

    d. Joyville

**3. What is the primary theme of Harmony's legacy?**

    a. Adventure

    b. Romance

    c. Unity and community

    d. Mystery

**4. What does the town of Harmony thrive on?**

    a. Solitude

    b. Vibrant traditions and close-knit bonds

    c. Modern technologies

    d. Individualism

**5. What does Ella witness in the town of Harmony?**

    a. The rise of technology

    b. The ebb and flow of life

    c. A decline in traditions

    d. Rapid urbanization

**6. What does the canvas of Harmony's legacy represent in the story?**

> a. A blank slate
>
> b. A masterpiece of growth and learning
>
> c. A representation of failures
>
> d. A town square

**7. What did the founding families contribute to Harmony's legacy?**

> a. Dark shadows
>
> b. Vibrant traditions and unity
>
> c. Modern technologies
>
> d. Individualism

**8. What were the golden fields of wheat a symbol of in the story?**

> a. Hard work and sustenance
>
> b. Economic downturns
>
> c. Failed harvests
>
> d. Unemployment

**9. What color symbolized love and passion in Harmony's legacy?**

> a. Green
>
> b. Red
>
> c. Blue
>
> d. Yellow

**10. What did the love stories under the ancient oak trees become in the story?**

> a. Threads woven into the fabric of the town
>
> b. Disconnected narratives
>
> c. A source of division
>
> d. Forgotten tales

**11. What color did red represent on the canvas of Harmony's legacy?**

> a. Storm clouds
>
> b. Failures

c. Moments of courage

d. Love and passion

## 12. What was green symbolized in the story?

a. Failures

b. New friendships

c. Storm clouds

d. Moments of courage

## 13. What challenges did the town of Harmony face, according to Ella?

a. Economic downturns, natural disasters, and losses

b. Economic prosperity and innovation

c. Unemployment and migration

d. Lack of education and enlightenment

## 14. How were challenges portrayed on the canvas of Harmony's legacy?

a. Dark, somber shades

b. Resilience and strength

c. As sources of despair

d. As insurmountable obstacles

## 15. What did the founding families build in the town of Harmony?

a. Schools and libraries

b. Houses

c. Modern skyscrapers

d. Factories

## 16. What did the youth of Harmony embrace, according to Ella?

a. Ignorance

b. Learning and intellectual pursuits

c. Disconnection from traditions

d. Entrepreneurship

**17. What did the azure hues represent in Harmony's legacy?**

a. Leadership and governance

b. Art and expression

c. Education and enlightenment

d. Romance

**18. What did the town square host in the evolved Harmony?**

a. Festivals celebrating the kaleidoscope of cultures

b. Silent protests

c. Large-scale construction projects

d. Political debates

**19. What did Ella marvel at in the transformation of Harmony's legacy?**

a. The decline in diversity

b. The rise of monotony

c. The loss of traditions

d. The mosaic of diversity

**20. What did Ella's eyes sparkle with pride about in the story?**

a. The decline of education

b. The rise of technology

c. The establishment of schools and libraries

d. The loss of intellectual pursuits

**21. What color represents the intellectual pursuits in the story?**

a. Yellow

b. Blue

c. Green

d. Violet

**22. What did Ella pass to the younger generation in the story?**

a. A physical torch

b. A symbolic torch of tradition and growth

c. A magic paintbrush

d. A key to the town square

**23. What did the night settle in with in the town square?**

a. Silence and darkness

b. Warm lights of lanterns and the laughter of children playing

c. Rain and thunderstorms

d. A sense of foreboding

**24. What continued to evolve in Harmony as described in the story?**

a. A chaotic mix of colors

b. A stagnant town

c. The canvas of Harmony's legacy

d. A dull representation

**25. What did Ella's voice become in the ever-expanding symphony of stories?**

a. A whisper in the wind

b. A loud proclamation

c. An eerie silence

d. A haunting melody

**26. What did Ella conclude about the legacy of Harmony in the story?**

a. It was a stagnant masterpiece

b. It was a fading canvas

c. It was a living testament to the interconnected lives of its inhabitants

d. It was a forgotten tapestry

**27. What did Ella believe the town of Harmony had the power to do?**

a. Destroy traditions

b. Inspire and leave an indelible mark on the hearts of its people

c. Wither away

d. Reject diversity

28. **What did the town square glow with in the night according to the story?**

    a. Darkness

    b. Warm lights of lanterns and the laughter of children playing

    c. Silence

    d. Despair

29. **What did Ella pass to the younger generation in the story?**

    a. A physical torch

    b. A symbolic torch of tradition and growth

    c. A magic paintbrush

    d. A key to the town square

30. **What continued to evolve in Harmony as described in the story?**

    a. A chaotic mix of colors

    b. A stagnant town

    c. The canvas of Harmony's legacy

    d. A dull representation

# POEMS TO ENJOY

## 1. Journey Unfolding

Life, a journey, unfolds its tale, A tapestry woven, a cosmic trail. Through valleys low and peaks so high, We navigate beneath the boundless sky.

Challenges met with courage and grace, In every heartbeat, a rhythmic chase. Embracing joy, enduring strife, Life's a symphony, the dance of life.

## 2. Sunrise Reverie

In the dawn's embrace, a canvas is spun, Golden hues herald a new day begun. Life whispers secrets in the morning breeze, A symphony of possibilities.

Each ray paints dreams on the canvas of morn, With every sunrise, a rebirth is born. In the quiet dawn, hope is rife, Life awakens with the sun's first stripe.

## 3. Echoes of Laughter

Life's tapestry, a patchwork of laughter, Echoes in moments, ever after. Giggles of innocence, pure and sweet, A melody making existence complete.

Through the years, laughter evolves, A chorus of joy, a tale it solves. In mirth and chuckles, we find relief, Life's grand comedy, a masterpiece.

## 4. Whispers of Time

Time, a river, ceaselessly flows, Leaving echoes where it chose. In its whispers, memories are spun, The tale of a life, second to none.

Seasons change, and so do we, A dance with time, an eternal spree. Embrace each moment, like a rhyme, For in the whispers, echoes of time.

## 5. Serenade of Sunset

As the sun descends, a serenade begins, A symphony of hues, where the day rescinds. Life's chapters painted in twilight's glow, Reflecting on the journey we undergo.

In the sunset's warmth, memories ignite, A kaleidoscope of color, a breathtaking sight. The day retires, leaving dreams in flight, In the serenade of sunset, we find respite.

## 6. Footprints in the Sand

Life's a shore where waves imprint, Footprints left, a testament. In sands of time, stories unfold, A journey written, a saga told.

With each step, we leave our mark, In the fading light or the growing dark. Footprints echo, a legacy planned, On life's shore, in the shifting sand.

## 7. Dance of Raindrops

Life, a dance in the summer rain, Where every drop sings its own refrain. A rhythm on rooftops, a sweet sound, Nature's ballet, in raindrops found.

Cleansing tears from the sky's embrace, Life mirrored in each droplet's grace. Dance with joy, dance away the pain, In the dance of rain, life's art is plain.

## 8. Echoes of the Heart

Within the chambers of the beating heart, Echoes of emotions, a work of art. Love's crescendo, passion's sweet refrain, Life's melody, an eternal chain.

In every beat, a story is told, A saga of emotions, tender and bold. Listen closely, for in each part, Echoes the rhythm of life's beating heart.

## 9. Embrace of Moonlight

When the day surrenders to the tranquil night, Life dons a cloak, bathed in moonlight. Silent whispers in the lunar glow, A lullaby sung as the night winds blow.

In the embrace of moonlight, dreams take flight, Guiding us through the mystic night. A celestial dance, a silver sea, Life's enchantment in the moon's decree.

## 10. Symphony of Silence

Life's symphony, not always loud, Sometimes found in silence, profound. In stillness, echoes of the soul, A timeless melody, making us whole.

Listen closely, to the quiet hum, A symphony in the spaces between drum. Silent notes, delicate and precise, Life's grand symphony in the embrace of silence.

## 11. Blossoms of Resilience

Life, a garden of petals, fragile yet bold, Blossoms of resilience, stories untold. In storms and sunshine, they unfurl, A testament to life's unyielding swirl.

Each petal holds a tale of strife, Yet, they dance gracefully, embracing life. In the garden of resilience, where stories bloom, Life's kaleidoscope in nature's room.

## 12. Wings of Imagination

In the realm of dreams, imagination takes flight, Life's canvas painted with colors so bright. Wings of creativity, soaring high, A journey into the limitless sky.

With every thought, a new frontier, Life's adventure in the atmosphere. Imagination, the compass, pointing true, In the boundless skies, dreams renew.

## 13. Seasons of the Heart

Life, a cycle of seasons, forever in motion, Spring's hope, summer's devotion. Autumn's reflection, winter's repose, Each season, a chapter that life bestows.

In the heart's landscape, emotions play, A symphony changing with every sway. Through seasons of the heart, we find, Life's kaleidoscope, ever refined.

## 14. Echoes of Wisdom

Life, a scroll etched with wisdom's ink, Words of experience, thoughts that link. Echoes of the wise, timeless and clear, Guiding us through each passing year.

In the whispers of the sage, Life's lessons turn each page. Wisdom's echo, a lantern bright, Illuminating the path in the darkest night.

## 15. Song of Solitude

Amidst the quietude, life finds its song, A melody soft, where souls belong. In solitude's embrace, whispers of peace, A refuge where life's clamors cease.

A song of self, sung without refrain, In solitude, life's truths are plain. A tranquil tune, a lullaby, In solitude's song, echoes of the sky.

## 16. Harbor of Memories

Life, a harbor where memories dock, Sailing through time, with each tick of the clock. Ships of laughter, anchored in the bay, Memories that forever will stay.

In the harbor of yesteryears, stories unfold, A tapestry of memories, a treasure to hold. Anchored in the harbor, safe and sound, Life's memories, in stillness, are found.

## 17. Echoes of Gratitude

In the whispers of gratitude, life unfolds, A symphony of thankfulness, stories told. Each note a blessing, a heartfelt grace, Life's richness found in a grateful embrace.

Echoes of thanks, like a gentle breeze, In the forest of life, among the trees. Gratitude's melody, a soothing balm, In life's tapestry, a cherished psalm.

## 18. Labyrinth of Choices

Life, a labyrinth where choices entwine, Pathways diverging, a complex design. Decisions made, a maze to explore, Each choice knocking on destiny's door.

In the labyrinth of choices, we find our way, Navigating through night and day. The echoes of decisions, a winding rhyme, In the labyrinth of life, a dance with time.

## 19. Aurora of Possibility

Life, an aurora painting the night sky, Colors of possibility, reaching high. Dancing lights, dreams to ignite, A celestial canvas, a breathtaking sight.

In the aurora of possibility, dreams take flight, Illuminating the darkness, banishing night. Life's potential, a radiant display, In the aurora of possibility, we find our way.

## 20. Elegy of Endings

Life's journey, an elegy of endings, A symphony where fate is sending. Chapters close, yet echoes remain, In the tapestry of loss, we find gain.

In farewells whispered, memories bloom, Life's poignant melody, a song of the tomb. Endings, a prelude to beginnings anew, In life's elegy, resilience is true.

# TRY THE RIDDLES

1. I speak without a mouth and hear without ears. I have no body, but I come alive with the wind. What am I?

2. The more you take, the more you leave behind. What am I?

3. I fly without wings. I cry without eyes. Wherever I go, darkness follows me. What am I?

4. The person who makes it, sells it. The person who buys it never uses it. What is it?

5. What has keys but can't open locks?

6. The more you take, the more you leave behind. What am I?

7. I have cities but no houses, forests but no trees, and rivers but no water. What am I?

8. What comes once in a minute, twice in a moment, but never in a thousand years?

9. The more you take, the more you leave behind. What am I?

10. I can be cracked, made, told, and played. What am I?

11. What has a heart that doesn't beat?

12. The more you take, the more you leave behind. What am I?

13. I have keys but open no locks. I have space but no room. You can enter, but you can't go inside. What am I?

14. What has an endless supply of letters but starts empty?

15. What has a head, a tail, is brown, and has no legs?

16. The more you take, the more you leave behind. What am I?

17. What has a heart that doesn't beat?

18. I can be long or short. I can be grown or bought. I can be painted or left bare. What am I?

19. What begins and has no end?

20. What has an eye but cannot see?

21. The more you take, the more you leave behind. What am I?

22. What has a heart that doesn't beat?

23. I have keys but open no locks. I have space but no room. You can enter, but you can't go inside. What am I?

24. What has an endless supply of letters but starts empty?

25. I'm not alive, but I can grow; I don't have lungs, but I need air. What am I?

26. What has a heart that doesn't beat?

27. I can be cracked, made, told, and played. What am I?

28. The more you take, the more you leave behind. What am I?

29. What has a heart that doesn't beat?

30. I have cities but no houses, forests but no trees, and rivers but no water. What am I?

31. What has an endless supply of letters but starts empty?

32. What has a head, a tail, is brown, and has no legs?

33. I speak without a mouth and hear without ears. I have no body, but I come alive with the wind. What am I?

34. What begins and has no end?

35. I have keys but open no locks. I have space but no room. You can enter, but you can't go inside. What am I?

36. What has an endless supply of letters but starts empty?

37. What has a heart that doesn't beat?

38. The more you take, the more you leave behind. What am I?

39. What has a head, a tail, is brown, and has no legs?

40. What begins and has no end?

## ANSWER THESE QUESTIONS ON LIFE-

1. What is the meaning of life?

2. Why do we dream?

3. How does laughter make life better?

4. What makes a moment unforgettable?

5. Can you measure the value of a smile?

6. How does music touch our souls?

7. Why do we feel a connection to nature?

8. What is the essence of true friendship?

9. Why do we find comfort in storytelling?

10. How does kindness change the world?

11. What role do challenges play in personal growth?

12. Why do we seek love and companionship?

13. How does forgiveness set us free?

14. What is the impact of gratitude on our well-being?

15. Why do memories shape who we are?

16. How does curiosity fuel our exploration of life?

17. Can a simple act of kindness create a ripple effect?

18. Why is there beauty in diversity?

19. What is the source of human resilience?

20. How does empathy build bridges between people?

21. Why do we find solace in art and creativity?

22. What makes a moment "perfect"?

23. How does hope sustain us during difficult times?

24. Why is it important to cherish the present?

25. What lessons can be learned from failure?

26. How does humor lighten the burdens of life?

27. What role does love play in overcoming obstacles?

28. Why do we find joy in the little things?

29. How does the pursuit of knowledge enrich our lives?

30. What is the impact of generosity on the giver and receiver?

31. How does the passage of time shape our perspectives?

32. Why do shared experiences create strong bonds?

33. What is the significance of finding one's purpose?

34. How does the beauty of simplicity enhance life?

35. Why do we seek moments of solitude?

36. What role does intuition play in decision-making?

37. How does gratitude transform challenges into opportunities?

38. Why is resilience essential for navigating life's journey?

39. What is the value of reflection in personal growth?

40. How does the pursuit of happiness lead to a fulfilling life?

# SYNONYMS OF WORDS RELATED TO LIFE

- **Challenge** - Adventure
- **Adversity** - Hardship
- **Triumph** - Victory
- **Pinnacle** - Summit
- **Journey** - Odyssey
- **Strive** - Endeavor
- **Resilience** - Tenacity
- **Persevere** - Persist
- **Ephemeral** - Fleeting
- **Serendipity** - Fortuity
- **Resplendent** - Radiant
- **Ubiquitous** - Everywhere
- **Voracious** - Insatiable
- **Euphoria** - Ecstasy
- **Zenith** - Apex
- **Nadir** - Lowest point
- **Epiphany** - Revelation
- **Quintessential** - Pinnacle
- **Precarious** - Risky
- **Serenity** - Tranquility
- **Epoch** - Era
- **Dichotomy** - Duality
- **Vicissitude** - Change
- **Pertinacious** - Persistent

- **Exuberance** - Enthusiasm
- **Equanimity** - Calmness
- **Resonate** - Reverberate
- **Cacophony** - Discord
- **Nostalgia** - Sentimentality
- **Ethereal** - Otherworldly
- **Mellifluous** - Harmonious
- **Peregrination** - Journey
- **Labyrinthine** - Complex
- **Mellifluous** - Sweet-sounding
- **Ephemeral** - Transient
- **Ineffable** - Unutterable
- **Vivacious** - Lively
- **Ineffable** - Indescribable
- **Panacea** - Remedy
- **Ubiquitous** – Omnipresent

## ANTONYMS OF WORDS RELATED TO LIFE

1. Simple - Complex
2. Easy - Difficult
3. Light - Heavy
4. Soft - Hard
5. Joyful - Sorrowful
6. Smooth - Rough
7. Carefree - Worrisome
8. Gentle - Harsh
9. Flexible - Rigid
10. Pleasant - Unpleasant
11. Harmony - Discord

12. Free - Restricted

13. Comfortable - Uncomfortable

14. Tranquil - Turbulent

15. Peaceful - Chaotic

16. Clear - Confusing

17. Generous - Stingy

18. Open - Closed

19. Frugal - Extravagant

20. Safe - Risky

21. Flexible - Inflexible

22. Honest - Deceptive

23. Genuine - Fake

24. Transparent - Opaque

25. Love - Hate

26. Build - Destroy

27. Advance - Retreat

28. Begin - End

29. Connect - Disconnect

30. Include - Exclude

31. Create - Destroy

32. Grow - Shrink

33. Awake - Asleep

34. Thrive - Decline

35. Accept - Reject

36. Succeed - Fail

37. Constructive - Destructive

38. Support - Oppose

39. Win - Lose

40. Construct – Demolish

# ONE WORD SUBSTITUTION ON LIFE

1. Serendipity - Discovering joy by chance.

2. Jubilation - Expressing happiness in a lively manner.

3. Resilience - Bouncing back from challenges with strength.

4. Vivacity - Full of life and energy.

5. Panacea - A solution that addresses all problems.

6. Euphoria - A feeling of intense happiness and excitement.

7. Zenith - The highest point of life's achievements.

8. Mellifluous - A sweet, harmonious life experience.

9. Pinnacle - The peak of success and fulfillment.

10. Equanimity - Maintaining composure in the face of life's ups and downs.

11. Epiphany - A sudden realization that brings profound understanding.

12. Quiescence - A state of peacefulness and tranquility.

13. Ubiquitous - Present everywhere, making life diverse.

14. Exuberance - Overflowing enthusiasm and joy.

15. Salubrious - Promoting health and well-being in life.

16. Paragon - A perfect example of a life well-lived.

17. Joie de vivre - A cheerful enjoyment of life.

18. Ineffable - Indescribable joy or beauty in life.

19. Renaissance - A revival of life and creativity.

20. Utopia - An ideal, perfect state of life.

21. Ascendancy - A position of dominance in one's life.

22. Luminosity - Radiating light and positivity in life.

23. Halcyon - Calm and peaceful, like a perfect moment in life.

24. Quotidian - Simple, everyday pleasures in life.

25. Zen - Achieving a state of calm and simplicity.

26. Symbiosis - A mutually beneficial relationship in life.

27. Mellowness - A gentle and relaxed quality of life.

28. Epoch - A significant period in one's life.

29. Sanguine - Optimistic and positive outlook on life.

30. Jubilant - Filled with joy and celebration.

31. Felicity - Intense happiness and joyfulness in life.

32. Traverse - Navigating the journey of life with purpose.

33. Plenitude - A state of fullness and abundance in life.

34. Halcyon - Tranquil and carefree times in life.

35. Ebullient - Overflowing with enthusiasm and excitement.

36. Apotheosis - The highest point of divine perfection in life.

37. Resplendent - Shining brilliantly with beauty in life.

38. Zenith - The highest point or culmination in life.

39. Enthralling - Captivating and spellbinding experiences in life.

40. Sempiternal - Eternal and everlasting joy in life.

## SENTENCES WITH WORDS ON LIFE

1. Ubiquitous - Everywhere

- Happiness is ubiquitous in a garden full of blooming flowers.

2. Ephemeral - Short-lived

- The beauty of a rainbow is ephemeral but leaves a lasting impression.

3. Serendipity - Pleasant surprise

- Their encounter at the bookstore was a serendipity that led to a lifelong friendship.

4. Mellifluous - Sweet-sounding

- The mellifluous melody of the piano filled the room with warmth and joy.

5. Equanimity - Calmness

- In the face of challenges, she maintained equanimity, inspiring others with her composure.

6. Quixotic - Idealistic

- His quixotic dreams of changing the world drove him to pursue a career in philanthropy.

7. Sycophant - Flatterer

- The politician was surrounded by sycophants who praised every decision, regardless of its merit.

8. Resilience - Toughness

- The tree's resilience allowed it to withstand even the fiercest storms.

9. Panacea - Universal remedy

- While exercise is not a panacea for all health issues, it certainly contributes to overall well-being.

10. Vicarious - Indirect

- Through reading, she experienced vicarious adventures in far-off lands.

11. Pernicious - Harmful

- Gossip can have a pernicious effect on relationships and trust.

12. Alacrity - Eagerness

- With alacrity, the team embraced the new project and worked tirelessly to achieve success.

13. Mellowness - Softness

- The mellowness of the sunset painted the sky in warm hues.

14. Lethargy - Laziness

- Overcoming lethargy, she embarked on a daily exercise routine to improve her fitness.

15. Serenity - Peacefulness

- The mountain lake exuded serenity, providing a tranquil retreat for those seeking solace.

16. Epiphany - Revelation

- During her travels, she had an epiphany about the importance of simplicity and gratitude.

17. Quotidian - Daily

- The poet found inspiration in the quotidian moments of everyday life.

18. Salubrious - Healthy

- Living in a salubrious environment can positively impact both physical and mental well-being.

19. Esoteric - Obscure

- The professor's lecture on quantum physics was filled with esoteric concepts that left the students bewildered.

20. Mellifluous - Pleasant-sounding

- The mellifluous laughter of children echoed through the playground.

21. Querulous - Complaining

- His querulous attitude made it challenging to work with him on group projects.

22. Ephemeral - Fleeting

- The beauty of cherry blossoms is ephemeral, lasting only a few weeks each spring.

23. Ameliorate - Improve

- Volunteering can ameliorate the lives of those in need.

24. Nonchalant - Indifferent

- Despite the chaos around her, she remained nonchalant and focused on her work.

25. Redolent - Fragrant

- The kitchen was redolent with the aroma of freshly baked cookies.

26. Pantheon - Group of gods

- In ancient mythology, the pantheon consisted of various deities with distinct powers.

27. Incandescent - Glowing

- The incandescent glow of the lanterns lit up the night during the festival.

28. Quixotic - Idealistic

- Despite facing numerous setbacks, his quixotic pursuit of world peace never wavered.

29. Facetious - Humorous

- His facetious remarks lightened the mood during the tense meeting.

30. Ineffable - Indescribable

- The view from the mountaintop was so breathtakingly beautiful that it was ineffable.

31. Ebullient - Enthusiastic

- The team's ebullient celebration reflected their excitement about the project's success.

32. Magnanimous - Generous

- Displaying a magnanimous spirit, she donated a significant amount to the charity.

33. Languid - Lethargic

- The hot afternoon left everyone feeling languid and in need of a siesta.

34. Nebulous - Vague

- The instructions were nebulous, leaving the students confused about the assignment.

35. Diaphanous - Transparent

- The diaphanous curtains allowed soft sunlight to filter into the room.

36. Zenith - Peak

- His career reached its zenith when he received the prestigious award.

37. Ephemeral - Momentary

- The joy of winning the championship was ephemeral but unforgettable.

38. Insouciant - Carefree

- With an insouciant attitude, she approached challenges with optimism and ease.

39. Ineffable - Unutterable

- The beauty of a starry night was ineffable, leaving the observers in silent awe.

40. Epitome - Perfect example

- The elegant ballroom dancer was considered the epitome of grace and skill.

# CASE STUDY QUESTIONS ON LIFE

### Case Study 1: Balancing Act

Emma, a 35-year-old professional, finds herself struggling to balance her demanding career, personal life, and self-care. She is often stressed, feeling overwhelmed by the constant juggle. Her health is starting to suffer, and she's unsure how to regain balance.

- What are the key stressors in Emma's life, and how might they be affecting her overall well-being?

- Suggest strategies and lifestyle changes Emma could implement to regain balance in her life.

- How can Emma prioritize self-care without compromising her professional responsibilities?

- What role can support systems, such as friends, family, or colleagues, play in helping Emma achieve a healthier balance?

- Explore potential long-term consequences if Emma continues to neglect her well-being.

### Case Study 2: Life Transitions

John, a recent retiree, is finding it challenging to adjust to his new life after decades of a structured work routine. He feels a sense of loss and is uncertain about how to redefine his purpose and daily activities.

- What emotional challenges might John be experiencing during this life transition, and how can they impact his mental health?

- Propose practical steps John can take to navigate this transition and discover a new sense of purpose.

- How can John build a fulfilling daily routine that fosters a sense of accomplishment and well-being?

- Explore the role of social connections in supporting John through this life transition.

- Discuss the importance of maintaining a positive mindset during major life changes.

## Case Study 3: Coping with Loss

Sarah, a 40-year-old mother of two, recently lost her husband in a tragic accident. She is struggling to cope with the grief and support her children through this challenging time.

- Identify potential stages of grief that Sarah might be experiencing, and how they manifest in her daily life.

- Suggest coping mechanisms and support systems for Sarah to navigate the grieving process.

- Explore the impact of grief on Sarah's ability to parent and ways she can support her children.

- Discuss the role of professional counseling or therapy in helping Sarah cope with her loss.

- Consider long-term strategies for Sarah to rebuild her life and find a new sense of purpose after the loss.

## Case Study 4: Meaningful Aging

George, an 80-year-old retiree, is determined to live a meaningful and active life during his golden years. However, he faces physical limitations and occasional feelings of isolation.

- Assess the potential physical and mental health challenges that George might encounter as he ages.

- Propose lifestyle adjustments and activities that can enhance George's overall well-being and sense of purpose.

- Explore the importance of social engagement and community involvement in promoting healthy aging.

- Discuss the potential role of technology in helping George stay connected with others and maintain an active lifestyle.

- Address the significance of maintaining a positive attitude and adapting to changes for a fulfilling life in the later years.

Take life a
little less
seriously.
You'd enjoy
yourself a
lot more.

LIFE
IS TEN PERCENT WHAT HAPPENS TO YOU
AND 90 PERCENT HOW YOU RESPOND TO IT
LOU HOLTZ